Dog Training

Complete Guide to Training Your Dog or Puppy to be Obedient and Well Behaved

Renee Harvey

Table of Contents

Renee Harvey

Introduction

I want to thank you for buying this book, "Dog Training: Complete Guide to Training your dog or puppy to be obedient and well behaved" and sincerely hope you find it useful.

Dogs are a man's best friend but they require the right training just like kids do in order to be successful members of a family. There are multiple movies and books that tell us how loyal dogs are to man. These dogs need to be trained to be well behaved and this takes patience and understanding. This book gives you the entire procedure to follow to train your dog to be a well behaved dog. This guide tells you how to train dogs of any age. The methods used in this book are very simple and proven to work.

You will find step-by-step procedures that you will need to follow to train your dog. It tells you how to train your dog to sit, heel and any other action that is required. Every relationship needs to have great communication and you need to be in control of this communication. You will be able to communicate easily with your dog through obedience training. Once you are able to communicate with your dog, you will find that your dog will be well behaved and a credit to you.

Before I even start talking about dog training, the first step is to identify what type of dog you are going to get. Do not buy a dog based on hearsay or for their good looks but choose one that will blend in with your lifestyle. Remember, a dog is not something you should buy on a whim. Every breed has its own personality and inside of this personality, each dog has its own sub-personality. For example, you may want a dog that is always around no matter what, to cheer you up or you may want a dog to help you to feel secure. Maybe you want a dog that has a delightful personality and makes a great family pet. In any case whatsoever, a dog is not any benefit to your family if it is not properly trained or you do not pay attention to the initial training needed to make that dog behave in a manner that is acceptable.

Once you decide what personality of dog you want, you can then research and choose a breed of dog that fits the bill. The next thing is getting the dog to learn and blend with your lifestyle. Having said that, do not let the size of a dog deter you from choosing it. If you feel you will not be able to manage a big dog, but it is the dog that will manage you, this book is exactly what you require.

By the time you reach the end of this book you will be confident enough to manage and train almost any dog to blend in with your lifestyle. So without any further ado, let us get started and get your new friend trained.

Thank you once again for buying this book and I wish you the best with your training. Remember that it takes patience and as long as you have ample patience and a lot of love to give to that animal, he will give so much back to you through loyalty as the years go by. Then you can really enjoy being a dog owner and he will equally respect your home and your family and become a very valuable part of your family life.

Renee Harvey

Chapter 1
Choosing a Dog

There is much more to choosing a family pet than walking into a store and picking out a pretty dog. Each breed of dog has its own base temperament. Not every type of breed is meant for every type of person. This is because each type of breed requires a specific type of personality in order to create a well-behaved, obedient dog and a partnership between owner and dog.

Researching the Perfect Dog

In order to choose the right dog, you must be willing to do some research into the various personalities that each breed has. It is important to take the time to understand the various issues regarding each breed, just as it is important to truly reflect upon your needs and your household in order to determine what type of dog would fit best.

Renee Harvey

Many people make the mistake of choosing a dog based on what they believe the perfect dog to be. However, it is important to be fair to the dog that you are planning to get and ensure that it will in fact make a great fit for your home. For example, if you have a one bedroom apartment, it would not be fair to a Great Dane to try and cram him into the tiny space you have. Not only would the dog be uncomfortable and be tempted to get into trouble, but you would probably have a very difficult time training him because he has too much pent up energy.

The things you should consider when you are contemplating whether you should get a certain breed of dog are:

- The amount of space you have

- The breed's energy level

- The amount of maintenance the breed requires

- The basic temperament of the breed

- The recommended amount of exercise the breed requires

- How large the dog will get

- Your time constraints and how much time you will be able to spend exercising the dog

- Whether the breed requires constant grooming

- Whether the dog is suitable for a household with small children

- Which animal suits the age of kids that you have?

Once you find the breed of dog you are considering, take into consideration the dog's individual temperament and energy level. You should also consider how responsive the dog is to the human voice and how much attention it has been given by the breeder, or the shelter that you are getting it from. Try and find out some background information as this gives a lot of clues as to how the dog sees humans and behaves toward them. A dog that has been mistreated, for example, will not have the same level of trust as one that has not.

Take some time and spend it with the dog and see if you like how he/she responds to you. Do not simply choose a dog based on what it looks like. This is the number one reason that people return dogs to the breeder or shelter – they do not take the time to get to know the dog before they take it home and then find that it doesn't fit in with their expectations of it.

Even though the interaction you have with the dog is limited, you can learn a lot about dogs in a very short period of time by just sitting with them and going through simple exercises. Even better, take them for a walk and see how they respond to you and your specific style of handling. Most good breeders or shelters will let you do this within the confines of the shelter they have and encourage interaction between potential owner and dog.

The only time this may vary is when you are dealing with taking on a puppy since the puppy may need time to adjust to being with someone different to the people that he/she has become accustomed to. In the case of choosing a puppy, look at the standard of care given to the dogs and hygiene of the kennels because this gives you a lot of clues. The puppy should of course be vaccinated and at the correct age to be bought so that it is not taken away from its mother prematurely.

Chapter 2

Everything You Need To Know About Training Your Dog

Most people believe in sending their dogs to people who have specialized in dog training or they hire personal dog coaches. What they forget is that by training their dog themselves, they are building a very strong bond between the dog and themselves that will last a lifetime. By training your dog yourself, you are teaching your dog to listen to you, and not a stranger. Even though someone else trains your dog to understand commands, they still need to become familiar with your commands, which may prove to be more difficult than simply training the dog yourself in the first place. Once you understand the mind of a dog, you will realize that no one can train your dog as effectively as you can and you will know exactly why.

Dog training is a process in itself; it is as simple yet important as teaching the proper behavior to your kid. Now you wouldn't hire a coach to teach your child to walk and talk would you? The same applies to the dog. As a dog owner, you should take the steps required to teach him right from wrong.

What Your Dog Needs From You

Many people want to show their dogs love and care. The truth is that dogs need to feel trust in their living environment and learn discipline before they receive love and affection. Dogs have a mentality that requires them to live in a hierarchy. Someone has to take the lead role in the family just like dogs would in a pack. If your dog sees that you are not willing to take that role, chances are that they are not going to listen to you. The reason they won't listen to you is because they have assumed the role of pack leader, a role that you refused to take in the first place. You have to make your role clear from the beginning and that's all part of the training.

While many people see taking the dominant role as not being a great pet parent, the truth is actually the opposite. Once you establish your role as a dominant leader, your dog will be more likely to listen to you and learn. Dogs don't understand affection in the same way as human beings and they need that security of knowing who is in charge.

14

So what does the dominant dog in a pack do?

The dominant dog does a lot of things that the lower pack members do not have the privilege to do. Why? Because this is how nature has set up the hierarchy of a dog pack, which is built into the natural mentality of every dog on the face of this planet.

Dominant Dogs:

- Eat first

- Lead the pack

- Have the final say

- Have the power to command the rest of the pack

- Have the ability to give love and affection when the other members of the pack have done well.

While it may be tempting to show your puppy or dog love and affection at all times, it is important to realize that in the natural order of things, a puppy or dog must first earn this love and affection from their pack leader, dominant dog or master. Otherwise, it sends all the wrong messages.

Many people are under the misconception that their dog must be a certain age to begin training. This is completely false. Their mother has already begun the training process before they were even weaned. This is why you will see the mother dog nipping at her puppies when they become too rowdy. So, if the mother dog has already begun training her puppies, why not pick up right where she left off? It makes a lot of sense and keeps their life more consistent.

If you have chosen not to get a puppy, and you have chosen to get your dog from a shelter, training must start from the moment the shelter hands you the leash. Older dogs can be trained, but may have already built up bad habits that need to be put in check. Remember, you may be testing the ground with owning a dog, but the dog is also testing the ground to see who the pack leader is. Don't fail at this juncture because it's important that the dog knows who the boss is.

Myths of Dog Training

Dogs need to be six months old before they begin obedience training

Like every other animal, a dog also must be taught right from the time he comes to live with you about what is right and what is wrong. If you leave it for the future, your puppy might pick up bad habits that will definitely be hard to get rid of. You can start training your puppy from day one, as it will be easier for the both of you in the future. So don't waste time wondering if it is too early, as there is no "too early" for puppy training. Start as soon as your puppy gets in the car and enjoy the benefits later. Inconsistency confuses a dog so if you are ultra-kind and forgiving in the first week, you may just have sabotaged your chances of being the pack leader in the future.

Treating the dog during training leaves him expecting more

This is false. When you are training, you must reward your dog for being obedient. You can always put the treats away once the training has been done. You can pull the treats out again when you want to teach your dog something new. Remember though, not everything should be rewarded with a treat. Some things can be rewarded with a simple petting or a little snuggle which will equally be viewed as a positive reinforcement and treat for the dog.

Older dogs do not learn new tricks

This is another myth that has spread extensively. Older dogs do learn tricks and can be trained quite easily. Dogs are intelligent animals and can grasp things at any age. It might be slightly difficult for older dogs since they may have learnt bad habits and need to be given enough time to learn news ones. In this case, the secret is repetition and consistency. Like any other animal, including man, a dog needs time to get over the habits it has been practicing repeatedly to be able to learn newer and more acceptable habits. However, bad habits should be nipped in the bud quickly and consistently. Your dog must know immediately that you are the leader of the house and that he must listen to you at all times.

The guilty look

Your dog might chew the door or scratch it with its nails when you are at work or away from the house for a couple of hours. Your dog might make an expression that would melt your heart. This is not the expression of guilt. This is a fearful look since your dog knows that you are upset over a scratched door. You must remember that your dog associates the scratched door and you together as bad and does not associate the action as bad because scratching is a normal behavior for a dog. The key is to teach your dog that scratching the door is bad. If your dog does this as a form of anxiety relief while you are gone, you should consider crate training him to prevent further damage.

We must pet our dog if he is nervous

This is something that most dog lovers inadvertently do. What they do not understand is that they are encouraging their dog to be nervous because he sees the pat as some kind of validation that he is doing something right. When you cuddle your dog when he is afraid, he thinks it is a reward for being afraid. It is far better to tackle what makes the dog fearful and show the dog that there is nothing to be nervous about once that trigger has been removed.

Dog Training Secrets

There are a lot of methods that go into training a dog. It is a tiring experience but one that helps you create an unbreakable bond between you and the dog. There are a few concepts that you should remember while training your dog. It makes it easier for both him and you during the training period. Most people do not consider these concepts to be vital but this is where they make a mistake. They need to follow through with these concepts to ensure that their dog is obedient and well behaved.

Precursor

The precursor is that incident which brings out a certain reaction from your dog. These incidents could be anything under the sun. You might not be able to identify the incident but you will find a difference in the way your dog is behaving. You need to recognize these.

Behavior and Consequence

The precursors elicit a certain kind of behavior from your dog. This behavior further elicits a response from you that becomes the consequence. For instance, your dog might be lying down quietly on the floor in the living room. When somebody knocks on the door, your dog becomes attentive and stands up.

If it is someone the dog knows, he might bound forward and began jumping on the person. This elicits a reaction from both the guest and you that is what the dog craves. What you must teach him is that if he behaves in such a manner, he is being restrained and not treated. You must teach your dog the difference between restraint and coddling. Repetition of an acceptable response helps, followed by reward when appropriate.

Timing

According to many sources, your dog takes approximately 1.5 seconds to identify the cause and the effect of an event. You must remember that all types of learning are at a maximum during these 1.5 seconds. If you miss the moment, you might end up losing the chance to either correct your dog's behavior or reward him for the same. This leaves your dog confused since he does not know what is correct. Similarly, if you punish a dog long after the sin he may have committed, he will not be aware why he is being punished.

Consistency

You must always remember to be consistent with how you train your dog. In school and college we always had a set schedule to follow. This helps us learn efficiently and quickly. A dog, in the same way, needs a schedule that he can follow. He will also need to be given the same rules and restrictions so that he remembers them fully and will never fail to follow them. If you allow a behavior to be followed at one point and reprimand it the next moment, your dog will be confused. Always stick to the same response to your dog's behavior no matter what the situation. An example here is giving scraps from the table. You can't do it one day and then tell the dog off for begging the next. It is contradictory and unsettling for the dog not to know what is right and wrong because your signals are not clear.

Reward

Like every other animal, a dog loves to be rewarded for what he does right. Sometimes your dog ignores the rewards. You must try to identify what appeals to your dog. A reward can mean anything from a toy to an ear scratch. Keep in mind, your dog does not see going for a walk in the park as a reward because in a case such as this, the dog does not know what he is being rewarded for.

Preventing Your Dog from Becoming a Nuisance Dog

If I could count how many times I have heard a dog owner say "he barks nonstop" or "he embarrassed me when he mounted the mailman's leg," it would certainly mount up. Inexperienced dog owners typically find something about their dog that they cannot stand and usually have a "my dog misbehaves" story to tell.

I have to admit that when I hear a dog owner start such a statement, I feel extremely disappointed and even a little bit sad. I feel this way because these dog owners have taken the time to complain, but they have not taken the time to see the problem from the dog's perspective. Basically, they do not take the time to understand their dog and what the problem is behind the behavior.

Simply put, dogs do not misbehave because they have a spiteful attitude, they are out to annoy you or because they want to make you mad. They are just behaving like a dog behaves.

Most behavioral problems that dogs suffer from that annoy the humans around them are not considered problems to the dog. They are a problem to the humans around them. Whether you know it or not, your dog has a reason for every behavior that the dog exhibits, whether the behavior is good or bad. But you came here to learn about how to train your dog so I will give you a few reasons why dogs do what they do.

- Dogs bark because they want to get your attention or they are alerting you to something.

- Dogs dig holes in the back yard because they smell something in or under the dirt and want to know what it is.

- Dogs chew up items around the house because they are teething or they are nervous.

- Dogs chase moving items because it is their instinct to do so.

- Dogs become aggressive because:

- They want to protect you

- They feel threatened

- They do not feel like someone has taken the alpha spot in the home

- The dog senses that you are not able to fulfill the alpha role in the pack

Essentially, dogs 'misbehave' because they have not been taught that the behaviors they are exhibiting are not acceptable behaviors. This is due to lack of care and training from their humans. There are a wide variety of reasons that behavioral problems may arise other than training issues and you should be on alert and look out for these before you automatically assume that it is an irreversible behavior issue.

1. Training – your dog needs proper training. Without it, he will feel as though life is a free for all. He will not know what you expect of him and he will not ever be able to make you happy. He will easily become a problem to you and other people in the neighborhood because you have not taken the leadership role that you need to take.

2. Health Problems – Health problems are responsible for at least 20% of all behavioral problems. A dog that is sick or in pain will misbehave in a wide variety of ways. If your dog acts out of the ordinary when he has always been a well-behaved dog, you should take him to the vet immediately.

3. Improper Diet – If you are not giving your dog the right type of food, or you are feeding him food that is too high in proteins, fats or carbohydrates, you may be causing your dog to be hyperactive. Things like sugars, starches and

similar ingredients should never be in your dog's diet, as they can cause severe behavioral problems. Make sure that you read the label on your dog's food and ensure that it is properly balanced and does not contain byproducts. If you are unsure of what food you should be feeding your dog, consult with your vet. It is important that you do not change your dog's food based on what is on sale that week. Make sure to keep your dog on the same food until it is time to change due to age. Remember that your dog needs different food at various stages in his life and ask your vet to supply you with relevant information.

4. Exercise - if your dog is suffering from a lack of exercise, he can suffer from a wide variety of symptoms. A dog that is not receiving enough exercise time is overall unhealthy and will be hyperactive. The dog may also exhibit behaviors that are considered destructive. Dogs need plenty of exercise according to their breed and this should be one of the factors that are considered before you think about getting a dog or a puppy.

5. Lack of Proper Leadership - it cannot be stressed enough that dogs need proper leadership. Among all of the things that can go wrong when you have a dog, lack of leadership is one of the most pronounced reasons that dogs exhibit

behavioral issues. Dogs can develop numerous behavioral issues when they do not feel that they have a strong leader. The most noticeable behaviors that are exhibited are aggression, destructive behavior, leg lifting, marking of territory, mounting of various objects – including people, excessive barking and more. This is why it is so important that your dog sees you as the pack leader of the house.

It is important   that you understand that all dogs can develop behavioral problems. These problems never develop randomly. All behavioral problems that a dog develops are as a result your dog and his environment, including you, his master.   Almost every behavior a dog can develop can be controlled or completely resolved.   It is up to you to put in the effort to   train your dog properly. It is even more important for you to understand that it is easier to prevent a problem than to cure the problem after it has developed.

Chapter 3
How Do Dogs Learn?

Dogs learn through repetition. They learn to pursue a behavior that elicits pleasant responses and avoid behaviors that do not. When they are rewarded for having performed good behavior they continue to do so. When their behavior is either ignored or they are not rewarded for the same, they choose to stop performing that behavior.

Most dogs learn through two techniques, the principles of **Classical Conditioning** and **Operating Conditioning**. Classical conditioning is based on the experiment that Pavlov conducted with dogs. Throughout the experiment, the dogs associated ringing a bell with food and, as a consequence, they salivated whenever they heard the bell. Operating conditioning is based on an experiment that was conducted by Skinner on pigeons. The pigeons performed a series of movements in order to receive food.

The first step that you need to take while training your dog is classical conditioning. You can use a whistle or a clap as a response. You will need to teach your dog to associate a clap or a whistle to receiving a treat. The treats can initially be large in size but will have to decrease in quantity over time. Since food is something that your dog needs, he will work for it if he has to. The second type of reward could be praising or playing. Once your dog has become accustomed to the methods, he might not look forward to food but might look forward to praise or playing in the backyard.

Operant conditioning is something that needs to be done over the course of time. Your dog must associate actions and rewards. For instance, you want to elicit a bark from your dog. You can open a bone packet in front of your dog and wait. Your dog will be waiting patiently and will realize that you are looking for a certain response from him after which he will get the bone. He might bark or perform other activities that you have shown him previously. Since you are looking at eliciting a bark from him, you will have to wait until he barks to actually give him the bone. Once he is accustomed to this, he will bark whenever he finds you opening a packet of treats for him.

Teaching Your Dog a New Behavior

Teaching your dog a new behavior or getting rid of a bad behavior are very similar. Your dog learns through repetition and through a consistent response from you. Your dog may try to test the limits here and there, just to see what he can get away with, but maintain your consistency and dedication to teaching him the behavior that you would like to instill in your dog.

Another thing to bear in mind is consistency. You are the leader and family members must respect that the dog takes orders from you. They can use the same patterns with a dog but it's vital that they do not confuse the dog by giving inconsistent rewards that confuse him.

The next chapters deal with the actual training process and should help you to decide upon who the leader will be and how household members behave toward the dog as this helps in the training.

Renee Harvey

Chapter 4
Beginning the Training

Before you begin training your dog, try to identify whether your dog has any issues with dominance or fear. If these precursors bring out a strange behavior or aggressive behavior you might need to consider help from a certified trainer. This isn't usual in puppies but may be as a result of a traumatic experience in the past. That's why it is so important to check the history of the dog, so that you have an idea of what he fears.

When you are training your dog, you need not worry about the age of the dog. You can train your dog whatever the age might be. It is very easy to train a puppy that is younger than six months. Puppies learn very quickly between 8 and 16 weeks. They are very impressionable and responsive and want to please and be rewarded.

The main idea about training dogs is to remember to have fun. This is far more important when it comes to training puppies. You need to learn to be patient too. Never move on from exercises until you are sure that your puppy is confident of the exercise that he is performing.

When it comes to training older dogs, you will need to remember that it will take time. Older dogs have already learnt habits and are used to performing these without being corrected. It is not difficult to train them. It takes time since the dog needs to get rid of the habit that he has been following and to learn better habits. Learn to be patient with the dog and only move on from the exercise when you are certain that your dog has understood it. Remember that practice is what helps a dog of any age remember an exercise.

There are many households that have more than one dog at home. The owners might wish to train the dogs together. This is not a great idea since there are many concerns that might arise. The dogs might get confused and might learn exceedingly slowly if trained together. Training each dog separately is what works best. Once you have gone over the basic training, you can work on training them together but they do need the basic disciplines to be instilled first.

Training Requirement

When you are training your dog, there are certain items that you can use to help you to make the training more effective. These items will give you better results over time.

- ## *Soft treats*

  Soft treats work at any age. Dogs look forward to being rewarded for good behavior. Look for the ones that might contain nutrients, as this will help keep your dog healthy. Avoid the ones that have artificial coloring and flavors added in. Soft treats should be nutritious and also be something that the dog likes. Don't expect all dogs to like the same treats.

- ## *Leash*

  A leash is to help you hold on to your dog while training. Dogs have a very low attention span and the slightest distraction will have them forget the training. If you are training your dog in the park, make sure you have a leash. Chasing animals fascinates dogs and that's a natural curiosity. If they find a bird, they may start chasing the bird and forget all about the training. A leash will help you hold on to your dog and prevent him from running away. Make sure you buy a good brand that uses soft materials and will not harm the dog in any way. You could even use one that is extendable so that when you want to give more leash to the dog, you can.

- ***Collar***

A collar is to give your dog a sense of belonging. He will know that he has a home to which he belongs when he has a collar. It also helps give you a sense of dominance over the dog. This might be a rule in some states as it is important for dogcatchers to know that the dog belongs to someone and if they don't see the collar then the dog may be impounded. You can have one custom made for yours and have his name on it along with the owners name and contact details. Tags for this can be attached to the collar.

- ***Bed***

A bed is another item that can be used as a reward. After a long day of training you will have to allow your dog to relax. In the same way as you need a break after training at the gym, your dog will need a break from training. He will need to rejuvenate to do better. You can buy a comfortable bed or make one yourself using an old suitcase or a crate and stuffing it with comfortable pillows and adding a blanket that he or she loves.

Tips for Training Sessions

As a student, you were accustomed to having a schedule that you followed during school or college hours. You knew when you would get time to relax and what classes you had. In a similar way, a dog also loves having a schedule to follow. You will need to make sure that you follow a similar pattern every day while training your dog. You might confuse him otherwise as mentioned above. Below are some quick points to help you have fulfilling training sessions.

- Remember to time the training session for fifteen minutes. Initially, start off with one session and gradually move on to three per day. Do not burden your dog into learning multiple activities as it might confuse him/her and the dog might not be able to perform any one activity effectively.

- Always train in an area with minimal distractions. Dogs have a very low attention span (1.5 seconds). They need to be trained in an area in which they are comfortable and also where it is quiet. This gets you better results.

- You need to make sure that your dog is well rested. It is advisable to give him an hours' rest before starting a training session.

- Use a collar and/or a leash while training your dog. This will help till he learns to respond to your voice.

- Training sessions should always take place before a meal. If your dog is full, he might want to sleep or might not be interested in the treats. Dogs are usually lazy and love sleeping. They can sleep for more than 16 hours a day. You will always need to find time before meals to train him, as this is a time when he will be more alert and open to learning.

Always use treats that appeal to your dog. These could be chew toys, bones or biscuits.

Chapter 5
Modules of Training

There are essentially five ways in which you can train your dog —
shaping, luring, capturing, modeling and molding.

Shaping

Shaping is teaching through "successive approximation." That is
the scientific term. Through shaping, you teach your dog a
desired behavior. You will need to reward the dog for every
successive approximation to the final behavior. For example, if
you want your dog to fetch a stick, you will first reward him for
having found the stick. You will then treat him for sniffing it. You
will then finally reward him for picking the stick up and bringing
it to you, as that was the desired behavior.

Luring

When you want your child to eat, you wave the spoon in front of the child. Your child follows the spoon and finally eats the food when you put the food next to his mouth. Luring works in the same way. You lure your dog into performing a desired action using treats in your hand. For example, if you want your dog to sit down, you will hold a treat in your hand and hold it at a certain height. Your dog will be waiting for the treat. Once he has understood what you want, he will sit and you can reward him for the behavior performed.

Capturing

Capturing is a method of self-learning for the dog. You will need to watch your dog carefully while this is happening. This method usually does not include any incentives while training. It is only after training that your dog will receive treats. For example, if you want your dog to lie down, you will just sit with him till he does. Once he does lie down without having to be lured into it, you can treat him for having done so.

Modeling

Modeling is a technique that has been used to teach a vast number of creatures certain behavior. Through this method, you can motivate your dog to do better. This method involves learning through watching. A dog cannot learn from a human being, so he tends to learning from other dogs. If you have two dogs at home, this method works best. If one of your dogs knows the behavior to a command and the other does not, treat the dog that follows the command. The dog that does not know will follow the command once he sees you treating the other dog.

Molding

Molding is a common technique that most dog owners perform. This method involves teaching your dog to perform an activity by assisting him physically. If you want your dog to lie down or sit, you can push him gently lowering his shoulders into a sitting position.

Renee Harvey

Chapter 6
Training Exercises for Your Pup

This chapter deals with the basic training exercises that you will need to train your dog into being obedient and well behaved.

Release Word

You need to make sure that your dog knows when the exercise is complete. You can use a one word command to let your dog know that the activity that needed to be performed is now complete. Use an upbeat and a happy tone when you use this word. You will need to follow this sequence to accustom your dog to the release word.

- Ask your dog to perform an action.

- Once he has performed the action, reward him for it.

- Say your release word and allow your dog to break the action he was performing. Remember to make sure that your dog only breaks the command when you say the release word. If he does listen to you, treat him so that he remembers.

Sit Command

Your dog will need to learn to sit when asked to do so. He might not be accustomed to your voice and may need time to get used to it. When you are working on the sit command, you will need three sessions to train your dog to sit when he hears you say '*Sit.*'

You can follow these steps to make it easier for you and your dog

- Hold your dog to your left using his leash.

- Since dogs learn best through treats, hold a treat in front of your dog.

- Raise the treat in a slight upward arc until your dog sits. Once he sits, treat him and immediately give him the release word.

- Repeat this session 15 times

- Follow this method for two sessions without using the command.

- On the third session, match the command to when your dog sits. Treat him and use the release word immediately. Once he has understood the command, you need not use treats to make him sit.

- If your dog has not understood that he has to sit when you say the word, you can accompany the word with a physical action. You can mold your dog into sitting while saying the word so that he understands.

Come Back Command

Training your dog into coming back to you when called is necessary for him. It plays a vital role in keeping him safe. The sequence for this command goes as mentioned below

- Hold your dog by the leash and hold a treat in the other hand.

- Once your dog is distracted, hold the treat close to his nose.

- Your dog will immediately turn towards you for the treat.

- Hold the treat high up so that he cannot reach it.

- Bring the hand with the treat down to your side and let your dog take the treat from you. This way he will know that he will be rewarded if he comes back to you.

- Once he has understood that he must come to you, use the word '*Come*' the minute he turns towards you.

- You need not always use a treat. You can move onto using verbal praise when your dog has understood the command.

- Make sure that your dog associates coming to you as a positive experience. If you call your dog towards you for punishment, he will become wary of you and fear you - resulting in a varied response from your dog.

Training Your Dog to Walk with You

Most dogs love walks. They do not walk with you but might pull on the leash and run. You will need to train your dog into walking with you. Once your dog understands the commands, you and your dog can share long pleasant walks.

- Hold your dog by the leash. Make sure that you have minimal distance between your dog and you. Hold a treat in your other hand.

- Call your dog and start walking. If your dog takes two steps with you, stop and reward him.

- Increase the number of steps you take together.

- If your dog begins to pull, or stays behind, stop and wait for him to come to you. Reward him for coming back to you too.

- Repeat this process 10 times to help your dog understand the command. Once he understands the exercise, you can accompany it with 'Let's walk.' Once your dog has associated the exercise with the command, reward him.

Sit – Stay

The '*Stay*' command is very useful as it ensures that your dog stays in one place. This is the habit of a well-mannered dog. You can teach your dog to stay in one place using the sit command. Once your dog understands the command, you can walk away and be sure that your dog will not follow till he is released. The sequence you must follow for this command is given below.

- Hold your dog by the leash with one hand while holding a treat in the other.

- Ask your dog to sit down. If he sits for 3 seconds, reward him and say the release word. Repeat this five times.

- Once your dog sits for three seconds, begin increasing the sitting time gradually. You can move up to ten seconds in the first session and gradually move up to a minute over consecutive sessions.

- Remember to reward your dog every time he sits for the required period of time. After he sits for one minute teach him to stay.

- Use the command '*Stay*' the minute he sits and waits.

- Once he has understood the command, you must train him to stay even when you walk away.

- Stand at your dog's side and use the command "stay." Move in front of your dog and wait there for three seconds. If your dog has not moved, reward him and release him. Repeat the same five times. Once he has understood this exercise, give him the command to sit and walk two paces ahead of him. If your dog has not moved, reward him and release him.

- Repeat the exercise five times and gradually increase the number of paces.

This exercise ideally takes 5 – 8 sessions but it varies depending upon the dog.

Down Command

This command is as important as the Sit or Stay commands. It helps in having a well-mannered dog around the house. This command helps you exercise a certain amount of leadership over your dog. Sometimes your dog might not willingly perform this action, as it is a subordinate posture. Your dog might react aggressively.

At such a time, you will have to contact a trainer to help you with your dog. You can use molding to help you with this command. The sequence to training your dog with this command is very simple, but it takes time to get the dog accustomed to the command. You can also teach your dog to stay using the down command. It is easier to have the dog lie down and wait instead of sitting at waiting since lying down is a comfortable position.

- Hold your dog on the leash and hold a treat in your other hand.

- Ask your dog to sit.

- Hold the treat next to your dog's nose and slowly lower the treat to the ground.

- Make sure that you perform the action slowly so that your dog is able to understand it.

- It is good if you also lower yourself while lowering the treat.

- Place the treat in between your dog's legs and wait for him to lower his head. If he does not do so, you can gently encourage him to put his shoulders down.

- Once he is lying down, you can treat him. Repeat this about fifteen times, so he understands that he is being appreciated and rewarded for following your command.

- Perform this same exercise for four sessions. In the fifth session you can teach your dog the command. When your dog finally lies down, immediately use the command '*Down*' to help him associate the action and the command.

Stand Command

The stand command is useful when you are trying to groom your dog. It also saves a lot of time at the veterinarian. It does not take long to train your dog for this command. The sequence to train him is as follows:

- Ask your dog to sit while holding him with the leash. Hold onto a treat in the other hand.

- Lower the treat to your dog's nose and hold it there for a second. Start moving the treat parallel. Make sure that your movements are slow so that your dog can easily follow the treat.

- Once your dog has moved into standing up, reward him and release him.

- Perform the exercise ten times.

- Gradually increase the time for which your dog has to stand.

- Once your dog begins to understand the exercise, you can use the command '*Stand.*'

- Make sure that your dog does not move when he is standing until he is released from the exercise. If he moves before you release him, perform the exercise again.

Other Useful Exercises

You can use the above commands to train your dog to perform other exercises. You can get your dog to sit at doors, wait to get into a car, stay outside a grocery store and much more.

Once your dog has understood the basic commands given above, you can use them to help you train the dog more extensively.

For instance, if you want your dog to wait outside the grocery store for you, you can use the command 'Stay' and walk into the store and finish your work. You can be sure that your dog will not move from his place. Make sure that it is only you that performs this exercise and that it should only be used in public when you are certain that your dog has understood the command.

You can also train your dog into sitting while greeting somebody. Instead of bouncing towards them, your dog should learn to sit and wait till he is petted. You can give him the commands to stand or stay and have him behave himself around strangers.

Once you train your dogs, you will be able to take them out anywhere without being worried by their reactions to the people or the surroundings that they will encounter. They will behave themselves and also listen to you whenever necessary.

You can teach your dog to do fun tricks when in the presence of others. You can use Molding to teach your dog to spin and shake hands with a person. Once your dog is accustomed to doing it with you, he will also listen to outsiders as long as he knows that you have permitted it.

Chapter 7

Basic House Breaking for Your dog

In the previous chapter, we read about the various commands that you can teach your dog. In this chapter, we touch upon the basics of house breaking.

What is house breaking? Well, house breaking refers to training your puppy to only pee at a designated place and not inside the house. Similarly, he or she must relieve himself or herself outside the house or at a designated place inside the house.

House breaking is better known as house or potty training and is meant to help you train your dog eliminate waste outside the house.

Dogs and puppies are like babies and it becomes easy to predict their waste disposal pattern. All you have to do is to observe your puppy and understand how he or she operates.

You need not worry about whether a puppy will respond to your training, as most puppies will be accustomed to the idea of being trained. It will be in their genes and you only have to make a little effort to train them. Their mother will train them from day one. You are just continuing this natural training.

It is easy to house train your puppy if you understand how it works. To help you understand it better, here is how you must look at it.

Puppies are trained right from their birth to remain as clean as possible. Their mothers will clean them once they are done eliminating and they are taught to never pee or poop where they sleep. So this helps them understand that they must not eliminate in the area where they have to sit, sleep or eat and they will not do it in these areas.

But that does not mean they will not do it in the rest of the house. They will not understand that **you** have to sit, sleep and eat in different areas of the house. They will eliminate in any corner of the house that is warm and away from where they sleep.

Most puppies love to pee or poop on carpets because they find it warm and they assume it to be grass. Since they would have been trained by their mothers to poop in the grass or outside, they will look for similar surfaces inside the house.

They will eliminate on the carpet even if there is an open yard with fresh grass as puppies will not be confidence about leaving the house. They also love corners, places with taps such as kitchens, dark places such as under the bed etc.

To help you keep your house clean, here are some things about house breaking that you must consider and then precede with the process in order to make sure your puppy or dog knows that eliminating waste indoors is not acceptable.

Who Should Train?

This is a very important question as the puppy might respond differently to different people in the house. Most puppies get extra attached to one person in the house. If this person trains the puppy then it will be useless. The puppy will not be able to relate to being trained and think that it is only being played with. This person might also not be able to scold the puppy. So when training is in progress, this person should not be around or else the puppy will not respond positively to the training. This is not the leader. This is a person they associate having fun with.

It is advisable for people with a high pitched voice to train the puppy, as they will respond better to it. Since women and children have high pitched voices, it is best that you get them to train the puppy or puppies. Puppies do not generally get too attached to the women in the house and so, it is best that you get your mother, sister, wife or girlfriend to do it for you. Puppies will respond even better to children and you can ask your child to help you train the puppy. Make sure that you supervise your child, as they might not know to do it by themselves.

When is the Right Time?

There is really no right time to train your puppy but it is best that you start immediately. That is, as soon as the puppy comes home. If you wait any longer, then the puppy might not get adjusted or may develop bad habits that are hard to break. Some people wait for as long as a month but this time might be too much. The puppy would have already started to eliminate and trained a little by his or her mother to only eliminate outside of the specific areas where they sleep. If you think that your puppy already knows a lot then you must only gently guide him or her. Don't try and train them again as they might get confused and might forget their training. The mother of the puppy may well have trained them well, so use the first day to establish what level of training is needed.

What are the Things to Consider?

The things that you must consider while training your puppy is as follows:

Breed

The first thing that you must consider is the breed of the dog. The dog breed is necessary to consider as training times can differ from breed to breed. If it is a small breed, then it might take you slightly longer and generally medium to large breeds take lesser time to train. There are some extremely smart breeds that can take a command easily and this will help train them faster.

Basic habits

Basic habits of the puppy need to be considered. This means checking whether the puppy has already been potty trained and whether it knows that it should run outside to eliminate, whether it knows to not dirty furniture, carpets etc.

Age

The age of the puppy needs to be considered. If you got the puppy a bit too late, then you might find it a little tough to train it. You might have to spend more time training it and for it to understand where to eliminate. You might have to teach it over a longer period of time. This might reduce if you get a puppy that is really young, as they tend to respond better to commands.

How long does it take generally?

House breaking can vary from puppy to puppy but generally it might differ between 2 weeks to 2 months depending on how you approach it. This time can be more or less depending on the puppy's learning rate. If the puppy is a quick learner then it might take less time. Just a month might be enough to house break certain puppies. But there might be toy breeds that will take a lot more time than that owing to not being able to control their urges, and it might take you anywhere from 6 to 8 months or even a year. But this can be rare and even toy breeds can learn within 6 months. The results you get depend upon your consistency and the level of training you are able to give them.

Do Results Last?

Yes. Many people think that it can be extremely tough to train a puppy especially if it is really young. They believe that the puppy will not be able to remember the training and might keep forgetting about it. But this is not true and once you train the puppy then they will not forget about it. They will make the effort to only eliminate in the designated area. They will not do it inside the house. You will not have to supervise them and they will understand that it is not right to dirty in the house especially when they have to live there as well. They will go themselves and if they need help, then they will let you know by barking or scratching on the door.

Once they grow up, they will develop bladder control and be able to control the urge to eliminate. They will not depend on anyone and will do it for themselves. Most puppies will be trained to eliminate when they are taken on walks and you need not be worried about them forgetting the habit as they grow up.

Do I Need Props?

Yes you might. You might need sprays that give off an odor that might help you train your puppy. These sprays are used in areas where you want the puppy to eliminate. They will smell it and know where to go. So you can spray it inside the bathroom and on the grass or the insides of the sand box etc. Make sure not to accidentally spray areas where you do not want them to go. If you don't want to buy a chemical spray then you can make a simple one by yourself. Simply place some water and some clove oil and spray it wherever that you want the puppy to pee. You might also need toys that make a sound to help them follow you. Make sure the puppy loves this toy, as it will be more likely to follow you.

As you know you will need a leash or a cage or a harness if your puppy is being a little difficult. If you don't want to use these then you can simply place the puppy in a room and lock it. Make sure you can still see the puppy and he or she can see you, as they might not understand it is training. Being alone can cause the puppy distress and it is not encouraged that you leave it unsupervised for any length of time. You also need to be aware of the puppy's need to eliminate and allow it freedom to do so in the right place when this need arises.

How Many at a Time?

Some professional dog trainers will be able to house break many puppies at a time. They will know exactly what to do. But it is very wrong to use any kind of force and it is important to house train one puppy at a time especially when you are not accustomed to dogs. If you do have two dogs to train, then train them separately or they may think that you are playing.

This might take some time and you may have to place them in separate rooms when you are training them. Just as you see that they are ready to go to the toilet, you can transport both to the same place. They might bark and cry for a few days but with time, they will understand that you are training them and they will not trouble you.

If you have more than 2 puppies, then it is best that you take the help of family members and get each one to train a puppy and do it in the same way that you are doing it. This will ensure that you have all of them trained effectively.

What about Older Dogs?

It is possible to train older dogs as well. It might be a bit difficult but it is not impossible. They would have already learned to eliminate outside the house but if they are brought to a new place then they might not know where to go. Most adult dogs will have a greater control over their bladder and will not need to go as regularly as puppies. They will also be much more predictable and you will not have to observe them for long to see a pattern emerge.

If you are having difficulty training an older dog, then you can try and leash or cage them for a few minutes after a meal and place them in the area where you want them to go. This will help them understand better. But make sure the leash is long enough for them to move freely. You must be present there to supervise. You must clap and applaud when the dog is eliminating, as it will make it understand that you are praising it for what it is doing. With time, your dog will be able to understand it better and will make efforts to eliminate in the designated place.

Will it be Expensive?

No. There is no need to invest any money in it. You only have to buy a few things that will not cost you much. Some people use a litter box while others use newspaper and move this closer to the door, eventually praising the dog when he gets the message that the outside is the place to go.

If you were to employ a professional trainer, then you would have to shell out a lot of money. It would end up being a very expensive affair and you would end up having spent a lot of money on something that you could easily do by yourself.

So housebreaking your puppy should not be seen as a very difficult or taxing activity and you must consider it as a necessary part of puppy or dog care.

Five Important Facts about House Training

House breaking your dog can be a chore in itself. However, there are some facts that will make housetraining your dog a lot easier.

Fact 1: It does not take any longer to train an adult dog than it does a puppy.

Adopting an adult dog can be very intimidating. There is always a question as to whether or not the dog has been housebroken before you got him. The first thing you need to understand is that no matter how smart an adult dog is, he does not naturally know that it is bad to go in the house. Dogs must be trained to go outside. While most adult dogs are trained to go to the bathroom outside, a dog that was raised in a cage, was kept outdoors, raised at a puppy mill or was not trained properly by their previous owner may not know that it is wrong to go in the house. You will need to house break them afresh, just as you would train a puppy. Adult dogs do not have to go outside as often as puppies, which will make potty training easier than it is with a puppy, but when they do have an accident, they will create a much larger mess. The first thing you need to do with puppies or a dog is showing them the terrain. They won't know where to go until you do.

Fact 2: Puppies Do Not Have a Lot of Bladder or Bowel Control.

A puppy that has not yet reached 20 weeks old will need to go outside at least once per hour. A puppy under the age of 12 weeks will need to go at least every 30 minutes and possibly more often than that.

For an older puppy, there is a general rule for figuring out how long he can go without going to the toilet. The way to figure out how long your puppy can go without needing to go is to take their age in months and add one. For example, a 4 month old puppy can hold it for about 5 hours and no longer. A small breed cannot hold it as long as a large breed. Therefore, your puppy's bladder and bowel control may vary depending on their age and breed.

When your puppy is asleep, he will be able to hold it longer. However, do not make the mistake of thinking that a puppy that holds it for 6 hours while he is asleep will be able to hold it for the same amount of time while he is awake. There is a huge chance that he will have an accident if you make him try.

Fact 3: Dogs like Sleeping in a Clean Area

If given a choice, your dog will not go to the bathroom where he sleeps. This is a natural instinct that dogs are born with. For example, dogs in the wild will not go to the bathroom in their den. They will go outside of the den to go to the bathroom. As their pups grow, they learn the same natural instinct of going outside to relieve themselves.

By giving your dog a den like environment, such as a crate, and confining him to the crate when you cannot keep a constant eye on him, you will ensure that your puppy will not learn the bad habit of going to the bathroom randomly in your house. You do not want the bad habit to start, and this is the most effective method of preventing it.

Fact 4: Dogs Preform Best When they are kept to a Routine Schedule

By setting a schedule for your dog to eat, you will help him to create a schedule for going to the toilet. If you do not give him a schedule and allow him to eat whenever he wants, you will not be able to predict when he needs to go outside. Along with feeding him on a regular schedule, you should also take him outside on a regular schedule. Dogs will always go first thing in the morning and after feeding and drinking.

Fact 5: Punishing a Dog for an Accident in the House is Pointless and Could Do More Harm than Good

When your puppy has an accident, he will not understand what you are upset about. This is because what you are upset about is in the past to him, even if it only happened a few minutes before. Your dog will believe that he is in trouble for what he is doing at the exact moment you get upset and will not understand that you are upset about the bathroom accident.

The last thing you want your puppy or dog to believe is that he is in trouble for sitting down and quietly playing or that he is in trouble for walking up to you and greeting your calmly.

Common Scents!

A dog, no matter how old he is, depends on his nose to find the bathroom. If any dog has gone to the bathroom inside, there will be a chemical scent left in that area that is almost impossible for a dog to resist. Because of this, you will need to ensure that there is no odor of urine or feces in the house before you begin to housebreak a new dog or puppy. This may involve scrubbing your carpet with an odor neutralizer so that any previous odors do not cause any urge for your puppy or dog to use the bathroom in the house.

When you are cleaning, you may find it better to use natural remedies for cleaning up dog urine that involve using vinegar or ammonia. Look on the Internet and see what alternatives are available. This advice is actually really BAD advice as the smell of vinegar and ammonia closely mimic the scent of dog urine. The only way to get rid of the smell of urine is to use baking soda, club soda or odor eliminating cleaners that can be found at a pet supply store.

Simply cleaning up the mess and scent of your puppy's mistakes is not enough. You must make the area smell like your pack. A dog that relates an area to its pack will not use that area as a restroom. This is why a dog that is not housebroken tends to run to a location in the house that is rarely used, like a spare bedroom.

To do this, you should spend time with your dog in the newly cleaned area for several minutes each day. All you have to do is simply play with your dog in this room for several minutes each day while sitting in the floor. After several sessions like this, your dog will have a scent that says, "This is a no-potty zone!"

The only disadvantage to this method is that you will not be able to mark every nook and cranny of your house. While this method is effective, it is more of a deterrent instead of a foolproof plan. In order to ensure that your puppy does not foul the floor, you must use multiple methods of teaching your puppy to potty outside.

Crate Training and Housebreaking Your Puppy

If you do not watch your puppy closely enough and let him run all through the house he will go wherever he wants to go and this is a real mistake. Instead of allowing him to run through the house and not learning boundaries you should keep him close. This will help him to learn where he can and cannot go.

Remember dogs do not like to go to the toilet where they sleep, so keeping your puppy confined can help teach him to hold it. This will allow you to control when he goes to the bathroom and this will be soon after you release him from his space.

The crate for a puppy or dog should be large enough for the dog to lie on his side, stand up and turn around in. Make sure there is not too much room because this may encourage him to go in a corner where he will not be lying.

Lay a towel or old t-shirt in the crate so that he can smell you and get used to your scent. Also line it with other things to make it comfortable.

When placing the crate somewhere make sure that it is not in an area that is high traffic or around other distractions. Make sure it is still near the family but in a quiet area.

If you choose to place your dog's crate in your bedroom make sure he likes the crate first. Also be warned that the first few nights he may wine or bark which can cause you a couple of sleepless nights. If he does not like the crate at first, try placing treats inside to get him happy and used to it. Also make sure you say the word "crate" so that he learns what it is you are talking about. If that doesn't work, place the treats in the doorway of his crate and slowly move them further and further in. This may help getting him to like his crate.

When the dog starts to get more comfortable with being in the crate begin to shut the door for a second or two after and open it. Repeat this a couple times. After you have repeated this a couple times, try shutting the door and feeding him some treats so that he gets even more used to his den.

Once your dog or puppy gets more into this, find something that will take him a while to chew on so that you can place it in there for him to chew on or give him a chew toy that locks a snack in it. Place it in the cage and shut the door so that he cannot get to it. When he wants the door open or wants to be in with it tell him the words "crate" and let him in. If he goes in, shut the door and give him praise for going in. Leave him in the cage until he finishes his treat and open the door for him to let him out. If he has a chew toy that holds a snack take it so that he cannot carry it around with him. This will teach him that it is only for the crate.

Now refill the chew toy and tie it to the inside of the cage. When he decides to go in and play with his chew toy to get the treat out he may lie down and finish it, staying in the cage. Even if he doesn't stay in, close the door before he finishes the last of his treat.

If the puppy begins to get sleepy, make sure to try and encourage him to go to his crate by using the treats and saying the word "crate." Once he gets in the crate, close the door. If he has already fallen asleep move him to the crate gently and close the door.

This is a great way to help them to learn to use their crate when they are tired and also when it is time to go to sleep at night but it must be repeated so that they get used to it. Some puppies will take longer to get used to it and others you may need help by placing a sheet over the crate so that it will help to calm them down and fall asleep.

If your puppy begins to whine, do not let them out at first or you will teach them that they can do this regularly to get themselves out. This will lead to more trouble in training them where to sleep.

Most puppies will only whine for a little while before calming down and going to sleep.

If your puppy begins to whine when he has been quiet for a little while, he may need to go out to the yard for a pee. Don't let him out until his whining has paused. Again you do not want to let him know that just his whining that will get you to open the crate. Instead, if he is still whining make a noise that will interrupt him. Make sure to wait so that he doesn't start whining right away and if he does not, then open the door. When you let him out make sure to take him straight outside.

If you cannot watch your puppy or cannot have him outside or it is nighttime use your crate.

Do not use your crate for any punishment this will lead to your puppy not liking his cage and associating it with bad things and punishment. This will make things very difficult at sleep time or night, or when you are out and about and cannon watch him.

If you follow these steps, after a few days you we have a happy puppy that will love his den that will make him feel cozy and happy.

It's all in the Timing

Timing is what makes house breaking most successful. The goal you should have for your puppy is for him to be outside when he needs to go. Having him inside when he needs to go and not taking him out will not help in the training of your puppy.

You can easily predict when your puppy and his limited bowel and bladder control need attention.

When a puppy takes a nap and first wakes up, he will probably need to poop or pee right away. If you think he will need to go and you have something you need to get ready for, than you can wake him up early and take him out.

Rewarding your puppy is another key element to housetraining. When your puppy does something that shows correct behavior you should reward and praise him immediately. This will train him that when he does something that is correct he gets rewarded and he will continue to behave correctly.

Step-By-Step Housebreaking Process

You should restrict your puppy to these three types of situations to ensure that he does not have accidents in the house.

1. Indoors, constantly supervised

2. Outside in the yard with you

3. In their crate or den area

Your puppy should spend most of their inside time in their crate or den area while they are being house broken.

You will notice that there is not an option that includes your dog being left outside constantly. There is a large percentage of the population that believes puppies will be less trouble if they are kept outside. They feel this way because the puppy cannot pee or poop in the house, and they won't require constant supervision. The truth is that puppies that are allowed outside for long periods of time without a human within eyeshot do not become housebroken. In fact, it often reinforces the exact opposite.

Puppies that are left outside unsupervised are the ones who tend to turn into annoying dogs. These puppies usually grow up to bark, chew, dig and eventually learn to escape from your yard. Also, puppies who are kept outside typically become so excited on the occasions that they are let in the house, that the pee without warning. Because of this, these puppies are eventually isolated to the outdoors permanently and are no longer allowed to come into the house. This is the last thing that you want and if you are getting a puppy because you want it to be part of your family, then that's the last thing you should encourage.

So, how do you housebreak your new little furry companion? The next section of this chapter will explain the foolproof method of housebreaking your little fur-baby.

Fool Proof House Breaking for Your Pup

1. **Decide where you want your dog to use the restroom.** It may be helpful for your dog if you choose a potty spot that is somewhat close to the door. This will ensure that you do not have to go very far in order for him to go. Having a potty spot that is near the door will help when it is clean up time, especially if you have a large yard. It will also help by isolating the potty to one spot in the yard. This is extremely important if you have children and you don't want them to worry about random landmines in the yard.

2. **Learn when your puppy needs to go.** Until your puppy reaches a time when he can alert you to when he needs to potty, you will need to be an expert in reading his body language. At times, your puppy may need to go outside within 5 minutes of going out the first time. This is extremely important because it is detrimental to your puppy's training if you assume that you do not have to watch him because you just brought him in from going to the toilet.

Here is when you will need to take your puppy outside to go potty:

- Right after he wakes up

- Right after you let him out of his crate

- Every 30 minutes to 1 hour when he is awake

- After he eats

- After he drinks

- If he is chewing on a toy and gets up and begins looking around

- If he starts sniffing the floor

- When he goes to an area of the house or room where he has gone to the toilet previously.

- When he begins running around and becoming more excited than usual.

- If he begins wandering around near the door.

- If he begins pacing, whining or begins trying to squat. Keep in mind that male puppies will squat just like a female until they are between 4 to 9 months old.

- Ensure that your puppy is constantly supervised or in his crate when he is inside. It only takes a couple of seconds for your puppy to decide to squat and pee. This means that you should keep a very close eye on him. This does not mean that you have to stare at him, as this will make him extremely nervous. However, keeping an eye on him will let you know when your puppy needs to go to the toilet.

It also helps if you confine your puppy to one room. Unfortunately, you cannot wash dishes, watch television or go to the basement while you are potty training your puppy. Times like this are when you will need the puppy's crate to prevent accidents. If you do not crate him when you cannot pay attention to him, chances are that your puppy will have an accident. Any accidents that happen during this time are your fault, not your dogs.

- You should take your dog to his outside potty area every hour, or when he shows signs that he needs to go, whichever is less, and teach him to go on command.

- Every 30 minutes to 1 hour, grab several treats and take your puppy outside to his assigned potty spot. The best way to get him excited about the concept of going outside is to enthusiastically call "outside, outside, outside." It is important to encourage him to go rapidly so that he does not stop and go potty while he is headed outside. Also, rushing him along can help get him excited that will jiggle his bowels and bladder. This will ensure that he really needs and wants to go when he begins sniffing his toilet spot. Use words that he responds to. In our house, we use the word "Cat!" which always made the puppy head for the door, thinking that there was a cat there. It was a trick that worked.

- You should always use a leash, even if you have a fenced in yard. This will help you lead him to the right place and get him used to going potty while on the leash. This will make it easier to train him to potty while you are out on a walk. That's another good reason to have a collar that a leash can easily be attached to.

- Make sure to take your dog out at least once per hour. This practice serves multiple purposes.

- House train your dog in the shortest time possible.

- Teach him to use the designated potty area.

- Teach your puppy to go potty on command.

- Teaches your puppy to go pee and poop outside.

- Stand quietly and avoid staring at your puppy. If your puppy stares at you instead, it is most likely because he smells the treats you have. If this happens, just look away and ignore him. After a few minutes he will begin sniffing and getting ready to go.

    o   When your puppy does start to go to the toilet, quietly say, "Go potty." Ensure that you are using a tone that does not startle him or make him feel as though he is in trouble. You can use other cues, but make sure that you use something that you are comfortable using in public and that you do not mind your children using to describe your puppy's actions. This phrase should be used every time your puppy goes to the toilet because he will eventually learn to go potty on command.

- After your puppy has finished going to the toilet, immediately give him a generous portion of treats and a lot of happy, enthusiastic praise. The bigger the reward for going outside, the faster your puppy will train.

- The above mentioned steps are absolutely essential to potty training your puppy. If you were just to let your puppy outside and give him a treat when he returns to the house, your puppy's housetraining will take longer and will not be nearly as successful. Not only are you missing out on a chance to teach your puppy to potty on command, but also your puppy will think that he is being rewarded for coming inside, not for going to the toilet outside. Remember, puppies attribute what they are doing at the moment they are rewarded with why they are being rewarded.

- Make sure to spend time with and train your puppy! If you take your puppy outside and then bring him back in and ignore him, he will learn that after he goes to the toilet, his fun will end. This will make him more likely to avoid going to the toilet when he is outside and cause him to try and hold it longer.

To make training more successful you should take time to praise your puppy and take him for a walk as a reward. This extra reward will reinforce the behaviors that you are trying to teach your puppy and encourage him to go to the toilet quicker when he goes outside so that he can get the reward.

What if your puppy doesn't go when you take him outside?

If you take your puppy outside but he does not go with to the toilet in just a couple of minutes, take him back in the house and place him back in his crate. Try taking him out in another 10 minutes. Repeat these steps until your puppy decides to go. This will teach the puppy that he needs to go to the toilet when you take him out so that he can be let out of his crate. He will learn when and where to go to the toilet and again you will reward him and praise him for good deeds.

Should you put down newspapers?

When you let a puppy go to the toilet on a pad or newspapers, you may be making a mistake. This only reinforces that your puppy can do his business indoors and he may not bother to hold on until reaching the outside. This means that your puppy will never be housebroken or be able to hold it when the time is needed. However, if you do use newspapers, these are only really suited to tiny breeds. Holding a baby Chihuahua on a piece of newspaper until he pees may help to control the tiny bladder and a reward will reinforce that he goes onto the paper. Gradually moving this to the door helps him to see that as long as he does as he is told, he will get a reward. Eventually, the paper is taken away and is replaced by independently going outside the back door. This is only used in exceptional cases and for tiny breeds and that's the only advantage, since these breeds find it hard to control their bladder between the crate and the outside initially.

You can control what comes out by what he puts in.

Your puppy or dog, depending on the age, can be kept on a schedule. This can happen when you feed them on a regular schedule they will potty on a regulated schedule. You should only let your puppy or dog eat at certain times. Since puppies can potty as soon as 15 minutes after eating or drinking, if you allow your puppy or dog to eat when they want, you will not be able to predict when they will want to go. The same applies to snacks.

You should put food down for your puppy each day at the same time. Only leave it down for about 10 minutes and move it up out of their reach if it has not been finished. Puppies that are under 3 months should be fed 3 times each day; puppies older than 3 months and dogs should only be fed twice a day at set times.

Only give water at regular times but not after 7 p.m. Also watch how much the puppy or dog drinks so that you can decide more or less when he will need to use the potty. Also feeding them dry dog food instead of wet will also reduce the amount of liquid so that you can anticipate better when they will need to use the potty.

How to Handle Accidents

Fewer accidents will happen if you follow the steps we have gone over. As always accidents still happen. If there is an accident, make sure not to get mad or scold the dog. Take a step back and try to figure out why it happened. Maybe you were distracted or you just didn't take him out at the right time. Try to figure it out so you can try to keep it from happening in the future. It's usually down to the owner, or may be a sign that the dog is poorly.

Although may people think that dogs poop or pee out of spite when you anger them, this is not true. Dogs do not see this as a spiteful nasty thing to do to get back at people. When the dog cowers or shows guilt this is actually the dog submitting to the anger you are showing them.

Do not do anything if you do not catch your puppy in the act

Yelling, hitting, shaking or rubbing your puppy or dogs nose in it will not help to teach them. They do not see time the way we do. They will not understand any punishment given to them for something in the past even if it is just a few minutes ago. If you correct him for something done in the past he will think he is being corrected for something that is happening at this exact moment.

If you catch them in the act what can you do?

You can easily redirect your puppy or dog by creating a noise that will stop them in their tracks. This will allow you to quickly motion and call for him playfully outside. When you get him outside and he goes potty the way he should reward him again for redirecting himself the way you wanted.

You will also want to make sure you clean any and all accidents as soon as possible because if you don't, the scent will remind your puppy to try and use the same spot again.

How Long Before He's House broken?

Your puppy's age, size and your training will dictate the results and you will know when your puppy can be left alone and for what period of time.

It should only take about 2 months before you start seeing progress by following the guidelines shown for housebreaking your puppy.

As this all goes on, you can gradually leave him out of his crate more. This also depends on the dog. Some dogs will learn faster than others.

Dogs that are adults will usually need to go out about 4 times a day. Once in the morning, midday, afternoon, and before going to sleep at night.

If you think that there may be times you can't be home in time or are out longer than 4 hours you can look into getting a dog sitter.

In training puppies or even older dogs that have not been trained you must remember that there are going to be accidents. Remember that it is a process that has steps that need to be followed. Your absence will not help this.

Stay Alert for What May Happen

There are a couple difficult reasons that get in the way of housebreaking your puppy or dog.

If your puppy was bought from a pet store or puppy mill or even confined in a small space with no way to get out and go to the toilet, this could make for a difficult training. These puppies may require much more training before they get it since they have been brought up in a different way. Be patient and keep trying.

Another thing that can stand in the way is if you change the type of dog food or let them eat as much as they want. If you let the dog have too many treats or feed it off the table, then expect problems. This behavior can cause your puppy or dog to have diarrhea and also throw off their potty cycle.

Other reasons that can affect your puppy or dogs training could be physical. A urinary infection can make a big issue for training. Make sure to have your pet checked at the vet if you think that there may be an issue.

Chapter 8
Training a Dog with Aggression Issues

There is nothing more frustrating than bringing a dog home from the animal shelter or pet store and finding out that they have some sort of aggression problem. These aggression problems can range anywhere from barrier aggression – the fear of being in confined spaces - to food aggression and even resource aggression.

You may be wondering where the aggression began or what it stems from. Essentially, these are survival mechanisms that your dog had to develop in order to survive in the life he had before he became part of your household. There are ways to put a stop to aggression problems and return your dog to the happy-go-lucky pup that he was before he lived in a caged environment.

Removing the Aggression Focus

The first thing that you should do is focus in on the items that your dog is becoming aggressive over. Once you determine what your dog is showing aggression over, you should immediately remove this item from his surroundings. Keep in mind, removing the item from his environment is only a safety precaution. It does not actually solve the problem of aggression. Once you have removed the item or items that your dog is becoming aggressive over, you can then teach him how to control his primal instincts in a controlled setting. This is one of the most important steps, especially if you have children in the home. It also helps keep your dog from building a deeper aggression over these objects or events. The key is that you now have complete and total control over what is causing your dog's aggression and until he calms down, you alone have control over it.

Owning the Aggression Focus

Now that you have complete control over the focus of your dog's aggression, you can now reprogram the way he thinks about the object. Allow your dog to see you with the focus of his aggression, and know that it is yours. He cannot touch it. This may be food, water, a toy, bones, the crate or whatever else your dog has decided to be aggressive about. Your dog is now at your beck and call. If he wants his item back, he has to show you that he can be responsible with it.

Reintroducing the Aggression Focus

When it is time to reintroduce the aggression focus, you must do so in a controlled setting. This is especially true if you have children. The main focus of your dog's aggression should only be reintroduced when your children are within a safe distance and cannot get to the dog, or when your kids are in bed and they are safe from any repercussions of retraining the dog's behavior.

Food Aggression

Food aggression is one of the main complaints of pet owners and one of the number one reasons that dogs are dumped in shelters constantly. Many pet owners do not realize that this problem is extremely simple to solve and that it is essentially a break down in communication. This breakdown in communication may have happened before you got the dog. It is very typical of dogs that are in shelters and pet stores. This is because they are in confined spaces and must share what they get with other dogs.

If you think about the nature of a dog, you will realize that, in a pack setting, dogs are essentially loners when it comes to eating. The alpha dog gets the main portion of meat, while the lower dogs in the pack take what they need and drag it away from the other dogs to eat. In a home environment, dogs cannot do this. However, their mindset is still set to the natural way of life, until you take the position as pack leader and hand out his food accordingly.

The key to breaking the cycle of food aggression is to begin by forcing your dog to wait until after the entire family has eaten dinner. You ARE the pack leaders and your dog needs to be aware of this. After you eat dinner, it is your dog's turn to eat. Start by feeding him a small amount of food out of your hand. This shows that you own the food, both by putting your scent on the food, and by the action of you giving your dog the food. If he shows any sign of aggression, quickly remove the food from him, give a stern « NO » and walk away. After a few times of doing this, your dog will get the idea that you own the food and you have full control over his ability to enjoy his meal.

Once your dog has reached a point where he will happily take food from your hand, place about ¼ cup of food in a bowl. Put a small amount of food in your hand. Allow your dog to start eating from your hand and then dump the contents of your hand into the bowl. Once your dog is eating from the bowl, gently pat his head. If he shows any sign of aggression, use a stick to slide the bowl out of the way. Stand between him and the food with a confident demeanor. Pick the bowl up and place it on the counter. By standing between your dog and his food bowl, you are reclaiming the bowl as yours. You are essentially telling your dog that if he misbehaves, you have the power to revoke his meal. Walk away for about 20 minutes and try again.

Over time, your dog will get the idea that if he acts aggressively, you will take his food away.

Resource Aggression

Resource aggression is a condition in which your dog shows aggressive behaviors that are directly attributed to anything that can be considered a resource. This can be food, water, a corner of the yard, a toy, a cushion of the couch and many other things. Resource aggression, just like any other type of aggression, is a survival mechanism that dogs develop in accordance with their lifestyles. However, the sooner you put a stop to the aggressive behaviors, the better off you, your family and your dog will be.

With a dog that has resource aggression, you must remove all of the items that are causing your dog to exhibit aggressive behaviors. These items now belong to you, the pack leader. You can give them back to your dog one at a time but in moderation and only in controlled settings.

Once your dog displays any aggressive behavior, you must immediately say « NO! » and remove the item. Over time, your dog will learn that acting in an aggressive manner will cause them to lose the items that are extremely precious to them. More often than not, these behaviors will subside one by one when they see that losing their items will cause the item to become the property of the Alpha dog (you) if they act out.

Extreme Problem Behaviors (NILF) Training

If your dog has problem behaviors that are not remedied by simply removing the item and claiming it as your own, you may have to take an extra step in order to get your dog's attention.

Some people find that the "Nothing in Life is Free" program is mean and over the top. However, it is the best way to reinstate the concept of a pack and establish yourself as the leader of this pack, instead of allowing your dog to take over.

Nothing in Life is Free Training works basically the same as if you were grounding your child. Essentially, you take everything away from your dog, and they must do something for you in order to get their privileges back. The overall purpose of the dog undergoing this strict training is the same as your purpose in grounding your children. The overall goal with both is to take back control of your house and show that it is a give and take relationship, not simply a relationship where the dog takes and you give.

It is important to notice that not ALL behaviors that are aggressive involve a snarl, bark, growl or aggressive action from your dog. An aggressive behavior could be as simple as realizing that instead of you training them; they are actually training you to do exactly what they want you to. Don't believe me? Check out the problem that one of my clients had recently. While he did not realize that it was an aggressive behavior, his dog was challenging him as pack leader in a passive aggressive way.

~John was sitting on the couch reading his newspaper like he does everyday. This is John's time. After all, he had already put the kids on the bus, taken the dog for a mile run and now he was having time for himself on the couch. Rumples, his 4 year old Mastiff began bumping his leg trying to get his attention. John ignored him because he found the action to be intrusive. Rumples walked away and John went back to reading his paper. The next thing John knew was that Rumples plopped his ball directly in John's lap. John thought, "Man, he is being persistent." He ignored him again and went back to reading his paper.

The next thing John knew was that Rumples was sticking his head under the newspaper and demanding attention. Now, no matter what John tried, he could not read the story about what his neighbor was arrested for. Irritated and just wishing that Rumples would go away, John threw the ball. Boy does Rumples have John trained!

Once John realized what happened, he decided to turn to an expert to determine what he could do about a dog that basically runs the house and has spent months training John how to be a great human. He wanted the roles to be reversed and he wanted Rumples to listen to him, not just demand things from him. ~

The recommendation in this situation is to follow the Nothing in Life is Free training method, or (NILF). The NILF training is not really a program that centers in on specific problems that your dog has. Instead, it is a method of living with your dog that will address the main problem that your dog has. It is a method of building trust between you and your furry companion and a way to teach him that as long as he behaves well, he can trust you and accept you as his leader. You want your dog to be comfortable in his place in the family, which is definitely not as the leader of the pack.

One of the most dangerous things you can do, especially if you have a large dog, is to allow him to forget his place in the family. You also want your dog to be confident in his place as being a member of the pack and not the leader. You want him to know that as a regular pack member, he can live a comfortable lifestyle that does not deprive him of anything.

What is Nothing in Life is Free Training (NILF)
Your bartering point in this type of training is that you have resources that your dog wants. He wants food, he wants treats, and he wants toys and attention. These are all of the resources that your dog wants. The NILF program basically states that you control the resources that your dog needs. In order to get the

resources that you have, your dog must do something for you first.

This type of training may be something you are familiar with. While trainers call this method NILF, others call it "Say Please" and "No Free Lunch." Basically, these are just nicer ways of saying the same thing because they feel like the name that trainers use is a little harsh.

Practicing NILF

In order to successfully practice NILF, you must first teach your dog a few commands that they will need in order to be successful in the program. The most effective commands are:

- Sit, stay, down, come and heel are all great commands that will help you to reinforce this training with your dog.

- Stop simply giving your dog resources for free. Do you mindlessly give your dog a treat or pet him for no reason? Stop right now! Your attention and those treats are extremely valuable in the dog world. Do not give them away, make your dog earn what he gets.

After your dog has mastered a few basic commands, you will be able to start the NILF program with your pup. The first thing you MUST follow is before you give your dog anything or before you do something for them, they must perform one of the commands that has been learned. For example:

1. When you want to put your dog's leash on so you can take him for a walk, he must sit until you have his leash secure and you tell him to "come" with you.

2. When it is time for your dog to eat, your dog must sit and stay seated until you put the bowl on the floor. The main objective of this is to tell him "Okay" before he eats, essentially controlling what he does and does not eat.

3. When you want to play a game of fetch with your dog, you must make him do something for you before you throw the ball. An exercise like "sit" or "shake hands" works great for this type of situation. After your dog carries out the requested action, you can then throw the ball.

After you have given your dog a command, do not give him a treat, or whatever it is that he wants from you, until he carries out the action that you want him to. If he refuses to fulfill the action that you asked of him, be patient. Just remember that if your dog wants what you have badly enough, he will eventually give in to what you want him to do.

One of the most important aspects of NILF is to ensure that your dog is proficient in the command before you begin practicing this type of training.

What are the Benefits of NILF?

The NILF program requires your dog to work for everything he gets and keep his training up to date as much as possible. It is also a safe, positive and non-confrontation method of teaching your dog who the leader of the pack is.

Even if your dog does not bite, snap, snarl, or growl, he can still be very manipulative. Many dogs that pet owners complain about are overly affectionate – to the point of being pushy. Other dogs nudge you to be petted, wiggle their way onto the couch so that they can be as close to you as possible and many other actions that can get under the skin of their owner. By using NILF, you are gently reminding your dog that he lives in your house and he must abide by your rules.

Not only can NILF training bring an overly confident or manipulative dog back to ground level, but it can also help dogs that are extremely fearful to become more confident. As they learn new tricks, their success will increase their confidence level dramatically, eventually leading to a more comfortable, less stressed personality.

Why NILF Works

NILF works for three main reasons:

1. Dogs, just like humans, want good stuff. If the only way they can get what they want is by doing what you ask, they will do whatever it takes.

2. Positive leadership encourages good behavior rather than punishing for negative behaviors. By providing positive reinforcement teaching, you are providing guidance and boundaries that your dog needs.

3. Practicing NILF is a gentle and effective method of communicating with your dog that you are the leader that means that you have full control over the resources.

What to Do When Your Dog Has Developed Severe Aggression

If your dog has developed severe aggression problems, it may not be possible to train them on your own. In fact, it can be extremely dangerous to try unless you are properly equipped to do so. At times, a dog's behavior can become so severe that it requires the help from an outside trainer. Someone who is certified in training dogs who have developed problems with aggression that simply won't go away by using simple training methods. It is very rare that a dog that has aggression issues cannot be properly trained to respond appropriately in a family situation. However, it is extremely important to train your dog and maintain positive reinforcements to prevent behavior that is undesirable.

Renee Harvey

Chapter 9

How to Go About House Breaking

In the previous chapter we read about the basics of house breaking or potty training and looked at the things that you must know about it. In this chapter, we will look at the things that you must do in order to potty train your puppy and make him or her, a disciplined puppy.

Schedule

All puppies need to be put on a schedule. You must not feed your puppy as and when you like and must always give him or her food at the same time. The puppy's mother would have trained him or her to consume food at a particular time and it is best that you maintain the same routine. A puppy will remember the schedule for life and as it grows up, it will have a systemized routine and you will not have to worry about having to retrain your puppy when it grows into an adult dog.

The things you must maintain a schedule with include feeding, pooping, and peeing, cleaning, bathing, sleeping and playing. These are part of the training routine and are extremely important when it comes to house breaking. These will have a sort of chain reactions effect where the puppy will eat and then pee and poop and then sleep and then play and then eat and poop again. A systematic pattern will help it make easier for you as you will be able to predict his or her every little move and be prepared to train them effectively. This is all the more important if you have more than one puppy to train.

Feeding

Feeding your puppy on time is key. If you feed him or her as and when you think it is right, then your puppy will never respond to your training. You must make sure you give him soft food initially, as puppies will not be able to ingest hard foods and more importantly, they might find it tough to eliminate it. It is best that you soak any hard substance in milk or water to soften them and then feed it to your puppy even if it is puppy food. This is all the more important for small and toy breed dogs.

You must sit down and write the three food timings for your puppy and paste it on the wall so that you don't forget to feed him or her on time. You can also have reminders on your phone. If you feel the need to, then you can split your puppy's meals into 6 separate meals as opposed to three as this will help keep your puppy healthier for longer but might make it a little difficult to understand his or her elimination pattern.

Waiting

Remember that all puppies will eat and then poop. This pattern is well established, as they do not have a digestive system as elaborate as humans do. All they have to do is consume food and wait for it to push out the previous digested food. For this to happen, it does not take more than 15 minutes for large breeds and 10 minutes for smaller breeds. The exact time that your dog will take depends on his or her breed and the best way to determine it is by observing him or her for a couple of days.

Many people rush during this time but it is not important to do so. You rushing it will not help your puppy eliminate any faster and, in fact, he or she might get scared and might not want to eliminate in your presence. So keep calm and keep an eye on him. The tell tale sign that your puppy wants to eliminate will be when he or she starts circling around a small area. This they do even on the grass to help flatten it and when you spot this type of behavior, you can be sure that they want to poop immediately.

Action

After you spot this behavior, you must immediately spring into action and pick your puppy up straight away. Just make sure you don't press their stomach too much as this might cause them to eliminate sooner. They might feel slightly uneasy and so you must run outside the house. If it is inside the house like in the bathroom, then make sure you and the puppy are close as you can pick him up and run easily. When you run, make sure that your puppy understands what is happening. You can make use of words such as "poop" or "poo" which your puppy will start associating with the process.

You can then wait until your puppy is done and you must not rush it. You can take a seat and patiently wait until he or she is done. Most puppies like privacy so don't stare at him or her. If you want him or her to go inside the bathroom, then make sure you place them in the exact spot and not just inside the bathroom. It is best that you place the puppy on top of the drain plate, as it will be easy for you to clean the waste later. Outside the house, areas with grass or even a sand box are ideal. You can also have a sand box inside the house as you can easily cover the poop in sand and then throw it out of the house.

Supervision

After picking the puppy up and dropping it in the bathroom or the sand box, it is important that you teach it to run by him or herself. For this, you must start running as soon as the puppy starts to circle and encourage it to run with you. You must in fact start running a little prior to the circling, as the puppy might not get distracted when it has to urgently eliminate. Puppies will run behind children better and it is best that you get them to run with you as well.

Make sure you run and stand wherever it is that you want them to go and don't simply keep running around. Take the easiest route and avoid confusing the puppy. Don't pick him or her up again as they might develop the habit of being picked up and not learn by themselves. It is important that you run, as the puppy must understand the urgency of the activity. If you walk then it will not be able to understand that you are trying to train it to poop at a certain place.

Follow Up

Remember to always follow up. This means that you must teach your puppy to either rub his butt on the grass or you can spray some water to show how it is important to clean. Although the puppy will not be able to spray water, he or she might sit in a little water to clean their butt. This process will not make it tough for your puppy, as they would have been trained by their mothers to do the same. This is also important because your puppy might use your furniture and it is best that he be clean.

Using a tissue to wipe might not be right as it might only cause you to cause the puppy discomfort. If he or she is in the sand box, then you can simply roll the puppy's butt over the sand and then lightly dust it or encourage the puppy to dust him or herself. Just make sure that it is soft sand as harsh sand might cause your puppy discomfort. Although not necessary, you can dust his or her butt with a little talcum powder to help it remain dry and smell good as well.

Foods to Feed

Remember that you cannot feed your dog any kind of hard substance during the first 3 or 4 months. This will cause them to experience a lot of discomfort while eliminating and the puppy might not be able to concentrate on their elimination. This point is being repeated because most people don't realize that puppy food needs are similar to that of small children and end up feeding them all types of hard foods.

Even if the food meant for puppies is hard, you must soften it completely. This will also help the puppy eat food without having to chew, as they will not have teeth. You must not worry if the puppy will be able to eliminate solids and if it will become difficult for you to clean.

Within a week, your puppy will be able to eliminate solids and it will be easier to clean. You can use a sand box if you are worried or place the puppy right above the drain plate. But remember, once you train your puppy, then it will be impossible to train him to eliminate at another place. So think it through before you decide on a particular place. The outdoors is always preferable.

Leash

If you think your puppy is misbehaving in spite of you trying your best to train him or her, then it is best that you leash him or her. This will help discipline them. Make sure you leash them after they have their food and then pick them up and transport them to the bathroom after 15 minutes. This will help them understand that they are being disciplined and will start responding positively.

You must tie it again for another 10 to 15 minutes so that he or she understands that it is important to listen to you. If you do this at any other time and try and discipline them then it will not happen. They will not understand that you are trying to teach them to behave during house breaking. If the puppy falls asleep then don't disturb him or her and allow them to sleep and then release them to play. You can also make use of a cage if it is a small or toy breed and a leash might cause any undue stress. You can invest in a harness, as it will help take the pressure off of the puppy's neck.

No Punishing

Never punish your puppy by hitting or beating it. Remember that your puppy did not choose you and you chose him or her to be a part of your family. You must not take advantage of the situation and hit him or her if they do not respond to your training. They will not be able to associate the two actions. They will not understand that you are hitting them because they are not responding to your potty training. They might also get angry and create further problems. They might develop an aggressive nature and turn into puppies that get angry when touched.

Also remember to catch the puppy in the act. Some people make the mistake of hitting the dog or shouting at it after it is done doing the act. The dog will think that any mess is bad and not be able to understand that their poop or pee is the problem. So even if there is a mess on the floor like food or pieces of paper, then they will get scared of you, as they will associate your anger with the mess. So it is best that you catch them in the act and then show your anger in a very controlled way that they can understand.

Gradual Process

Don't think that once the puppy eliminates in the designated spot he or she has changed for good. You must continue training until he or she is completely trained. It will take some time for the puppy to understand and it might poop and pee inside the house a few times but you must not get mad and must always display patience. You must keep an eye on him or her throughout training and make sure that you follow the dog wherever it goes including under the bed, as that is the place that they love the most.

Celebration

Celebration refers to celebrating your puppy's new habit. You must always applaud and clap when your puppy does the right thing and you can give him or her a treat. This will help them remain inspired and look forward to pleasing you.

You can then have a small celebration party. This will help your puppy know that you are celebrating because they have done something right. Remember that dogs are social animals and they will love it that you have invited people to cheer for him or her. You can ask them to bring their pets along as well and this will help your dog meet with other pups. They will start to associate doing something right with being appreciated and make sure that they will obey you to have more celebrations.

Renee Harvey

Chapter 10

Making a House Puppy Safe

When you decide to indulge in training your dog, there are some important things that you must do in order to make it a pleasurable experience for both of you. This includes making your house puppy safe.

Making your house puppy safe refers to taking care of the several small things in your house that might be dangerous for your puppy. Many people make the mistake of thinking that the puppy will have enough common sense to not do something that will harm them. But this is not true. The puppy will only react to something but not be able to prevent something from happening. For example, if there is an open socket, then the puppy might lick it and get a shock. Here, it will react to the shock but not be in a position to prevent it by understanding that the socket is bad. It is the same as children. So you must take measures to have your house turned into a puppy safe environment and not simply take his or her safety for granted.

There are people who might think that their house is child safe and not make efforts to make it puppy safe. But remember that a puppy will be much more enthusiastic than a child and so you must try and make it as safe for them as possible. You will not have to invest too much money in it and it will only take a little effort from your side to make it safe for your puppy.

Remember, by making it safe, you will not just help your dog but also yourself from getting hurt as training might require you to do some running around in the house as well. You also will want to keep your valuables safe, as puppies will start to chew anything and everything that they think to be nice and chewable, especially when they start to teeth.

This activity is also known as pet proofing your house and might also be fine to do for cats and think of this as being part of the training routine.

Living Room

The living room is the first place that you must start with, as your puppy will access it more than any other room. You might also want to train it here as it is easier and you will spend a lot of time in the living room.

Couches

Puppies love sitting on couches and they will use it to train themselves to climb on high surfaces. So you do not want to keep anything valuable or breakable here, as they might jump on it and break it. You also do not want to have anything white or cream in color as the puppy will jump on it and make it dirty in no time.

TV unit

The TV unit might be the most expensive item in your house and so, you might want to keep it as safe as possible. Be sure to keep the television covered when not in use and if it is at a low level, then you might want to shift it to a higher level until your puppy grows up. Make sure the DVD player, PlayStation etc. are well hidden away so that your puppy does not get enthusiastic and start to chew on them or bite the cables.

Carpets

Carpets are something that will never be safe if you have a puppy in your house. If you have a new and expensive carpet, then it is best that you protect it or if it's a rug, roll it up and store it away. The puppy will want to pee on it and your carpet will be ruined. It is best that you not place the carpet back until the puppy is at least a year old, as he or she will love to chew on it when they start to teeth. The carpet might also be a hindrance when trying to train your puppy and so, it is best that you take it away for some time and keep it safe.

Cords/ wires

Any lose cords and wires in the living area will not be safe. The puppy will start to chew on them and you might have problems. Make sure you tie all these up and hang them up high, so that the puppy will not be able to reach them.

Tables

Tables are another thing that puppies love to chew on. If you have tables that have thin wooden legs, then your puppy will chew them. You might have a problem keeping the chair or table stable and it might collapse and cause further damage. It is important that you wrap foam around these and then cover it with duct tape. This will ensure that your puppy will not eat these things and your furniture will remain safe for a longer period of time.

These are the various things that you must do in your living room to make it puppy proof.

Kitchen

The kitchen can be full of dangers for a puppy. There can be a lot of things that can prove to be dangerous in general. You must puppy proof your kitchen effectively. Here are the things that you must bear in mind while puppy proofing your kitchen.

Gas stove

Gas stoves and cylinders are extremely dangerous with puppies in the house. You must make sure you keep these hidden and, more importantly, do not let your puppy near them. This is especially dangerous if the gas is on and there is something on the stove and the puppy is in the kitchen alone. If any hot substances slip and fall then it can cause the puppy great harm. Even if it falls away from the puppy, the puppy will get curious and might walk over it and burn its paws and licking it might cause it to have lip and tongue burns.

Utensils

Puppies will get curious with everything and that includes your utensils. If you have too many spare utensils lying around, then they will surely get curious and look into them and might also lick them. If you use these, then they might contain germs, as puppies would have licked a lot of other things. So it is important that you keep all your utensils and other such food containers on high platforms or hidden inside drawers. You must hang your pots and pans, as it will be beyond your puppy's reach even if it is a tall puppy.

Cords and wires

Cords and wires in the kitchen can be quite dangerous. It might also not be practical to tie these up, as you might need to use the full capacity of the cords. To solve this problem, you can have chew proof PVC tubes placed on the outside, which will prevent cords and wires from being bitten. If you are up for it, then you can have the wires completely replaced as this will help keep your wires safer for longer and also allow you to make these safe for yourself and your kids as well.

Foods

There are all types of human foods that can be toxic for your puppy so you must try and keep these away from him or her as much as possible. Here is a list of foods that you must keep as far away from as possible.

Chocolates and candies

Chocolates and candies are extremely toxic to dogs. These can cause your dog all sorts of problems and even a small amount can be harmful. So keep these as away and placed as high as possible to help keep your puppies safe. You may need to take extra precautions at Christmas!

Salty foods

Salty foods are bad for puppies. They will not be able to understand that these are salty foods. Place salt boxes and boxes containing salty foods at a higher level to help prevent puppies from reaching it. Do not let the kids feed the dogs on chips.

Snacks and junk

Snacks and junk foods will contain sugars and other chemicals that will not be suitable for the puppy. You must keep these away from the puppy as much as possible and ideally place them at high levels.

Onions

Onions are dangerous for dogs but they will not understand that. If they find a spare onion lying around, they will take it and start to eat it especially if they are teething. This is dangerous and so, it is best that you keep them as far away from your puppy as possible. If you have a vegetable rack, place this where the puppy cannot access it.

Coffee/ tea

Coffee and tea contains chemicals that can be dangerous for dogs. Milk is ideal for puppies and don't be tempted to add in any health drink powders as these will contain sugar and might also be chocolate flavored so be careful and keep them as far away as possible.

Tobacco and cigarettes

These are toxic for puppies. Make sure there are no packs available for the puppy to chew and discard used packs in appropriate dustbins that are placed out of their reach.

These form the various things that you must do in the kitchen to help make it fully puppy proof.

Bathroom

<u>Commode</u>

All puppies love to put their heads in the commode and might also drink from the bowl. This can be dangerous as the water might contain germs that can be harmful for the puppy. The puppy might get over enthusiastic and jump into the commode and that might be dangerous. If you have a commode that automatically flushes, then you might have to get that fixed and made non automatic or keep the lid closed at all times when the bathroom is not in use. That may be a hard habit for the men of the house!

<u>Tub</u>

The tub can be a very risky place for animals especially puppies. They will love to experiment and might jump in and break things. This can be dangerous and so, you must keep the tub empty at all times and drain the water as soon as you are done bathing. Make sure you do not let the puppy inside when the water is draining, as this can be bad for him or her as well. Be sure to not have any kind of electric wires close to the tub as well as this is common sense for any household.

Tubes

Your puppy might chew plastic pipes and this can mean trouble. The plastic might be dangerous for them and you might start to have leaks inside your house. To help solve this problem, have non chewable PVC pipes installed, which will prevent them from chewing and prevent you from having leaks and floods that might dirty your bathroom. It's actually best not to let a puppy into a place like the kitchen or bathroom when there is no one there.

Trash cans

Trash cans and bins in the bathroom can be quite dangerous for your puppy. There might be used razors that can be sharp and tissues that might contain germs. You must clear these out as soon as possible and not allow them to remain dirty for long. Place these cans and bins at a higher level in order to keep them away from the reach of your puppy or dog.

Bedroom

Closets

Closets can contain your expensive clothes and teething puppies are sure to get curious. They will chew on anything that they find to be perfect for their teeth and damage it. This includes collars, zippers, pockets etc. If you don't want your puppy eating these, then it is best that you keep them as hidden and locked away as possible.

Make sure that there are no spare clothes and rags that are lying on the floor. These might be dangerous as your puppy might chew on them.

Shoe racks

Puppies absolutely love shoes. They will chew all types of shoes regardless of shape, size, texture and color. If you have expensive ones, then it is best that you place them in boxes and keep them on a high shelf, or alternatively, keep the closet doors closed at all times. Make sure that there are absolutely no shoes lying around, as they might be dangerous. Get yourself a nice rack and arrange all your shoes on top and place it out of reach of the puppy.

Jewelry

Jewelry can be dangerous for your puppy. There might be small parts that can cause them harm if ingested. Make sure no jewelry is placed where your puppy can reach it and place all jewelry in boxes and inside your cupboards or drawers.

Cosmetics

Cosmetics including your make up, lipsticks, creams, nail polishes, nail polish removers and toiletries such as soaps, shampoos etc. should be as hidden away as possible. These can be highly toxic for the puppy and might also be very expensive.

Keep them stored away in safe places and out of your puppy's reach.

Garage

Paints

Paints in the garage will be highly toxic for your puppy. They might get curious and lick the can and that can be harmful. Keep your paints closed and as hidden away as possible. Never leave your puppy in the garage without being supervised and keep the garage closed at all times to prevent your dog from accessing it.

Cleaners

Cleaners such as phenols, bathroom cleaners, bleaches etc. must be stored on higher platforms and out of your puppy's reach. They might get very curious and drink these by mistake. So make sure they are in sturdy bottles having sturdy lids and are not in your puppy's reach as this might be extremely harmful for them.

Oils

Oils and greases can be toxic for you puppy. Ingesting even a little can be bad and so, make sure you place the bottles and cans as high as possible and away from your puppy's reach.

Tools

Tools in the garage are dangerous for your puppy and keep them in boxes. Make sure they are hung safely and the boxes have tight covers. If you think they need to moved then move them to the attic where the puppy is never allowed to go.

<u>Car exhaust</u>
The car exhaust can be dangerous. Don't allow your puppy in the garage when the car is inside. Make sure the doors are tightly locked and your puppy cannot access the garage from anywhere.

Garden

Many people don't realize that the garden can be just as dangerous as any part of the house and don't take measures to puppy safe their garden.

<u>Plants</u>
Plants can be toxic for your puppy. Some plants like indoor plants can contain chemicals that can cause harm to your puppy's mouth. You can find out about the different plants that are harmful for your puppy and try and keep these pots as far away from your puppy as possible. Do not have any inside your house even if it is in a planter that has been hung as the leaves might fall and your puppy might have access to them. Poinsettia is dangerous for dogs, so be aware of that at Christmas.

<u>Tools</u>
Garden tools can be dangerous for your puppy. Right from the fork to the spade, everything might be dangerous and so, it is best

that you keep these as hidden as possible or place them in a garden shed that is kept closed.

<u>Bugs</u>

Certain bugs in the garden might be toxic and your puppy might end up consuming them. Make sure you supervise your puppy at all times. If you see that your dog is eating something, then get the puppy to spit it out immediately.

<u>Soil</u>

The soil can contain lots of chemicals that can be bad for your dog. So make sure he or she is not eating any and that they are under constant supervision when they are in the garden.

Others

<u>Stairs</u>

Stairs can be dangerous for puppies. The staircase might cause them to fall down and injure themselves. You can make use of carpets to cover the stairs and perhaps even use a child gate to stop the puppy from going upstairs. This is especially important during training, as the puppy might have to fetch something and be curious about the stairway. If there is a lot of gap between the railings, then the puppy can get his head caught, so it's a better bet to keep the puppy away from stairs entirely.

Fireplace

The fireplace can be quite dangerous. Puppies will be attracted to anything that is lit up. So they might get curious and walk towards it. So make sure that the fireplace is covered and that there is no way the puppy can reach it. A good fireguard is a great investment.

Doors

Make sure you don't leave any doors open as the puppy might run out. It might be dangerous as the puppy may run out and not know where to go. It might also run out in traffic, which can be quite dangerous. If you have a door that leads out onto the street, then make sure that the puppy is supervised at all times.

Windows

High windows must not be left open, as the puppy might want to jump out, out of curiosity. Make use of wire mesh or even grills to help protect him or her.

Things Needed

Switch blocks

Switch blockers are what are placed on top of the socket to help cover them. This is important as puppies might be over enthusiastic and might try and slip their tongue into the sockets. This can be very dangerous and so, it is best that you use these in all the open sockets in your house. These are also great if you have small kids.

Cord ties

Cord ties can be bought anywhere and they are used to tie long cords and make them short and handy. Once you tie them, you can place them on higher platforms, as this will help keep them safe. You can choose them in the same color as the wires, as this will help keep them hidden and it will look more uniform. Make sure you secure them tightly as puppies will have a lot of energy and might jump up and try to chew them.

Boxes/ containers

Buy enough and boxes and containers to place all your tools and other things. Look at all the things that you need to box and then get the boxes and containers. You do not have to buy new ones and can only buy used boxes that can be bought from stores. Make sure you buy sturdy ones and place them as high as possible to help keep all its contents safe. Something you may want to box up until the puppy is matured are ornaments that they are likely to knock over.

Stair gates

Stair gates are what you can place at the beginning or top of all staircases. You can use them to keep your puppies from falling off the stairs. They can be bought from online stores and in child stores. It is best that you buy trusted brands instead of making your own as they are much more likely to be safety tested.

Fences

Fences can be used to fence larger areas such as the garden. Again, you can buy them in bulk to save money. Make sure that you have everything set up before your puppy comes home. Check the garden perimeter and see which areas need fencing to stop your puppy from escaping into your next door neighbor's yard.

Toys

Toys that you bring home for your pet need to be checked to see whether they are puppy safe. It is important that you choose toys meant for dogs or puppies. This means that you bring home only pet safe toys and not toys meant for kids. Your puppy's teeth will be very sharp and capable of piercing through even the toughest of plastic and so, it is important that you get rid of them. Keep all your child's toys in a container or box and make sure they are not thrown around and mixed with your pet's toys.

Remember that everything should be set up in advance and not after your puppy comes home. Before bringing the puppy home, check and recheck to make sure that all of your tools and extra materials have been put away safely. So plan everything in advance and have everything in place so that your puppy will not have difficulty adjusting and you can start with the training routine as soon as possible without hurdles getting in the way. Remember, puppies are curious, so give them nothing extra to be curious about.

Renee Harvey

Chapter 11
Things to Remember When Training Your Puppy

When you train your puppy or dog, remember that it should be as much fun for him or her as it should be for you. So don't make it a life mission to train them and make sure you enjoy the process. In this chapter, we look at the different elements and principles you must bear in mind when you train or discipline your puppy.

Dominance

Remember to establish yourself as the dominant person in the house. Your dog must revere you as someone who has the power of giving orders that they need to listen to. In order to do this, you have to show your puppy, or your dog, that you have power over the resources that they need on a daily basis. This will teach your puppy that you are now the pack leader and that they must do, as you want them to. For example, as pack leader, you have the power to tell them where to go to the toilet, or that chewing on the edge of the couch is not appropriate. No matter what other things exist on this list, dominance should be the first on the list and should be involved in anything else you do. Your persona as leader has to be established and kept in mind at all times.

Empathize

Remember to always empathize with your puppy. Dogs are smart no doubt but they will not be able to understand things as fast as you would. In fact, even children will not be able to understand as fast as you would. So think of it as being the same way you would teach children. You must understand that your puppy or dog will try his or her best to obey you and keep you happy. They will also empathize with you and understand that you are trying to train them. They will start to listen better when they understand that you are putting in a lot of effort to teach them something.

Remember, the more fun you have the more the training you will be able to effectively provide to them and they will enjoy it too. If you keep going at it without considering the puppy's limits, then there might be a lot of difficulty to face as the puppy will not be able to respond to your training and you may start getting angry. So make sure you think from the puppy's point of view and do not keep going without understanding your puppy's needs or his method of learning.

Friendship

Establishing friendship with your dog is very important. There can be temperamental dogs that might not be easy to befriend. They might not be interested in being friendly and so, it is up to you to establish friendship. You have to understand that they might need their space and so you must not force them to play with you or force them to be trained. This will further worsen the situation and you will not be able to establish a lasting bond.

It is best that you establish this bond by spending more and more time with them when they are young. Try and sleep with them, feed them their meal, play with them with toys etc. These things are sure to help you establish a lasting bond with your puppy.

You need not try and be over friendly as the puppy might get over pampered. Generally, over pampered puppies will not respond positively to your training. They will not understand that you are training them and will only be interested in playing with you all the time.

So make sure that you establish the right kind of friendship with your puppy and not overdo anything, as it will be crucial to help train them.

Renee Harvey

Patience

Patience is vital when it comes to training your puppy. You must display unquestionable patience, as it will help determine how fast your puppy will learn. If you start to get impatient, then your puppy will also get impatient. It will stop listening to you and start doing its own thing. You must make sure that the puppy is constantly listening to your commands and responding positively to your training. This patience should not just be during the training but also after the training is done.

You must help your puppy to develop patience as well. Placing his or her favorite toy in front and then shouting and saying "No" when he or she touches it can do this. If the puppy runs away with it, then you must take it back and place it where the puppy cannot reach it. You can then train it to develop patience again and not feel bad and give away the toy. This will cause the puppy to get used to it and he or she will not develop any patience. Making use of treats can do the same. You can place the treats in front of him or her but only let them have it after you say the command. This patience will help you raise a loving and caring dog.

Trust

Establishing trust is important for both you and the puppy. You must be able to help the puppy trust in you and you must trust the puppy. If you think your puppy will do something without

128

your knowledge, then it might get difficult for you to train him or her. You must make sure that the puppy understands enough not to do something that you do not like the minute your back is turned. For this, you must always catch the puppy or dog in the act and then scream "NO." This will ensure that they understand how you don't like something that they are doing and they will stop doing it immediately. Never do this five minutes later. It won't work.

If you stop them or scold them after the act is done, then they will not understand it and you will again start to have trust issues. Similarly, your puppy must trust you and should not be afraid of you. Some puppies might run away from their owners and refuse to come to them owing to having trust issues. Although their bad memories are short lived, they might remember some things for longer and be afraid to come to you. You must address this issue and start to win the dog or puppy's trust in order to train him or her effectively.

Understanding

Always be understanding when it comes to dealing with your puppy. This means that the two of you understand each other and know of each other's moods. Puppies will have moods when they will not want to play and will only want to sleep. If, at this time, you decide to play with the puppy, you will mess up the schedule.

It is important that you completely understand their schedule and then start the training to fit in with it.

Similarly, it is important that the puppy understands your moods. Most dogs are very clever and they will know when you are up for something and when you are not. But still, you must be able to teach them to understand your moods and only then will they be completely aware of when you are okay with playing, training etc. If this kind of a mutual understanding is not established then they will have a problem undertaking training and you might find it difficult to train them easily and effectively.

Enthusiasm

Enthusiasm is important when it comes to training your dog. Dogs will learn faster and better if you display enthusiasm while training them. If you make it dull and boring, then they will rapidly lose interest in it. They will not be able to understand that you are teaching them to train in something and take it as being just a boring activity.

You must make use of exciting words, tone, language, body language etc. They will not show interest otherwise and even if they do, then they will forget what you taught them easily. You may have noticed the way in which people use keywords when they are training and say them with enthusiasm. It's for a purpose.

But make sure you maintain consistent enthusiasm throughout. If your enthusiasm fades, then their enthusiasm will fade as well. They will stop responding to you positively and will not be able to learn fast. Many people start out with a lot of enthusiasm but lose interest rapidly. This must not happen, as it is important to maintain enthusiasm and not simply allow it to fade away as you go further into the training. Don't think of it as a chore, but as a bonding experience between you and your puppy. You must be excited about it until you complete the training and then you can be happy with your puppy or dog, which not only responds to you but also takes command well.

Strictness

When it comes to being strict, you must know when to be strict and when you can be lenient. If you are always lenient with your puppy or dog, then the puppy will not respond in the way that you want it to. Puppies will turn out to be spoiled pooches and you will have a tough time making them listen to you. They will also not be able to learn well and you might cause them to misbehave when strangers or other people are around. You might also have a dog that does not respond to potty training and dirtying or messing up areas of your house.

So don't be afraid to make use of your strict voice in order to train your puppy or dog. They will not get scared and will only take it as a signal for them to start behaving properly. As long as you do not hit your puppy or dog, just a strict and stern voice will not cause them any harm so don't be afraid to shout at them when you want them to behave properly. If you can't do it yourself, then get someone in the family to do it, as it is important to be strict with them wherever necessary.

Observance

Observing your puppy or dog's behavior is very important when it comes to training them effectively. Some dogs will have hidden talents and you will be able to make the most of them and use it to your advantage. Say for example you got a puppy whose parents were trained to walk on their hind legs. Some of those genes would have passed on to your puppy and he or she might walk on their hind legs even without you training them to. In such a case, you can encourage it and you will not have to train them too much to do it.

Similarly, there might be other hidden talents that you might not be aware of and so it is important that you observe your puppy or dog for a few days and then start your training session.

This can be even more important as you might have to plan your training depending on the type of talent that he or she has naturally and if you do too much and not train them the right way, then you might end up making them forget their inborn talents or confuse them and not allow them to do tricks properly.

Maintain Record

Remember to always maintain a record with your puppy's activities. This means that you must write down what you and your puppy did every day, as it will help you assess how much progress the two of you are making. You will be able to know if there is less progress or if there is the right amount of progress and be able to make changes to your training schedule. You can maintain a physical record of it or you can also maintain a digital record. If you do not have the patience to write every day, then simply prepare a planner and make sure there are tick boxes so that you can simply tick them.

You can maintain the same planner and use it for all your dogs. This will ensure that you get the best results with all of them and do not have to make a new one for them. You can also give it to friends and family as this will help them train their dog effectively and they will get to save on money that they need to pay for a trainer.

Never Give Up!

Remember to never give up. You never know when you puppy or dog might change and understand training properly. Some people give up very easily and only train their dogs for a few days before giving up. This is wrong, as the dog needs to be trained for at least a few months before it will be ready to take your command. If you feel like giving up, then take a small break from it and then start again. But make sure that this break is not too long.

The break will help you take some time off and also allow the puppy to understand what it was taught better. You will notice that your enthusiasm is back and so is your puppy's. Your dog will be able to learn it faster if your enthusiasm is really back again and you will not be disappointed with the results.

Conclusion

I want to thank you once again for purchasing the book and sincerely hope you enjoyed it.

In this book, I have discussed the intricacies of training your little pup, which in itself is a great bonding experience. Once you train your dog, you will be able to create a bond that will last a lifetime. It is best for you to train your dog yourself, as this will help you communicate with your dog. It will get you and your pup closer to each other and also help you understand each other in a better manner.

I hope the tips and tricks mentioned in the book help you successfully train your dog, without the help of a professional trainer. Again, training your dog is not rocket science but you need to have a lot of patience when you make an attempt to train your pup. With time, your dog will understand what you are seeking from him and will start obeying your orders.

Hope this experience turns out to be a fun bonding exercise for you and your pup. Have fun and good luck with training your dog!

Free Bonus Video: Dog Training 101 How to Train Any Dog the Basics

This is a MUST for anyone new to dog training, or anyone who has reached a plateau. Dog training should not be about domination, but communication. In this video here is some extra information to help you train your dog.

Bonus Video:
https://www.youtube.com/watch?v=jFMA5ggFsXU

Renee Harvey

34033796R00079

Made in the USA
San Bernardino, CA
17 May 2016